By Fumiko Takeshita

Illustrated by Mamoru Suzuki

Translated by Ruth A. Kanagy

The Park Bench, by Fumiko Takeshita, illustrated by Mamoru Suzuki, translated by Ruth A. Kanagy.
Text copyright © 1985 by Fumiko Takeshita. Illustrations copyright © 1985 by Mamoru Suzuki.
American text copyright © 1988 by Kane/Miller Book Publishers. Reprinted by permission of
Kane/Miller Book Publishers.

Printed in the U.S.A.

ISBN: 0-618-43600-6

23456789-QK-13 12 11 10 09 08 07 06 05 04

The Park Bench

ベンチが ひとつ

HOUGHTON MIFFLIN COMPANY
BOSTON

The day has just begun.

A white mist hangs over the park.

No one is here yet, and the park is very still.

Under a tree sits a single white park bench.

こうえんの　あさ。

きりが　しろい。みずも　しろい。

まだ　だれも　こない　こうえんは,

とても　しずか。

きの　したに,　しろい　ベンチが　ひとつ。

こうえんに　いちばんのりは、はやおきの　ひと。　たいそうを　する　ひと。いぬを　つれた　ひと。
しろい　ベンチも　めを　さます。　あ、いつもの　おじさんが、ちいさな　くるまで　やって　きた。

4

The early risers are the first to arrive.   Some do exercises. Others walk their dogs.

The white bench is just now waking up.   Look, here comes the park worker in his little motor cart.

5

"Good morning, my dear park bench,"
says the worker. "It's cleaning day for the
park," and he gives the bench a friendly
little pat.

Children pass by on their way to school.
Adults pass by on their way to work.
The town is becoming lively.

「やあ, おはよう, しろい ベンチ。
きょうは, こうえんを
きれいに する ひだよ。」
ベンチを ぽんと たたいて,
おじさんは, しごとを はじめる。

がっこうに いく ひとが とおる。
かいしゃに いく ひとが とおる。
まちが にぎやかに なって くる。

こうえんに，おじいさんが さんぽに きた。
つえを ついて ゆっくり。
はなを みたり，とりを みたり，
いそがないで ゆっくり。

「やれやれ，どっこいしょ。」
しろい ベンチで ひとやすみ。
「ちょうど いい ところに，
ちょうど いい ベンチが あるね。」

Here comes an old man taking his walk.

He moves very slowly, leaning on his cane.

He stops to smell the flowers and then to feed the birds.

He's not in any hurry.

"Now it's time for a rest," says the old man.

He sits on the white bench.

"The perfect bench in just the right place," he thinks.

Along comes a mother and her baby.

"Let's sit in the sun," she says.

"The white bench is bathed in sunlight."

"Da, da," the baby babbles.

"Goo, goo," the old man replies.

What *can* they be talking about?

つぎに　きたのは，あかちゃんと　おかあさん。

「ひなたぼっこしましょ。

しろい　ベンチに　おひさまが　いっぱい。」

ばあ，ばあって　あかちゃん。

ほう，ほうって　おじいさん。

ふたりで　なんの　おはなしして　いるの？

Friends meet at the park.

The two mothers begin to chat.

They talk on and on.

Chitter-chatter, chitter-chatter, until it's time to eat.

All the while the white bench listens quietly.

こうえんで　であったら,

すぐに　おしゃべり　ぺちゃくちゃ。

いつに　なっても　おわらない。

おなかが　すくまで　ぺちゃくちゃ　ぺちゃくちゃ。

だまって　きいて　いる　しろい　ベンチ。

It's lunch time. The park worker eats under a large tree.
Here come the cats and the birds.
"Okay, my little friends. I'll give you some food," he says.
"But, oops, don't make the bench dirty."

こうえんの　きの　したで,
おじさんの　おひる。
ほら, あつまって　きた
のらねこたち, ことりたち。
「よしよし, いま　わけて　やるからな。
おっと, ベンチを　よごさないで　くれよ。」

ひるやすみの　こうえん。いろんな　ひとが　くる。「ひるねには　やっぱり，この　ベンチが　いちばん
いいや。」　ふんわり　そよかぜが　いい　きもち。　ベンチも　いっしょに　うっとりする。

During the noon hour, lots of people come to the park to relax. "This park bench is my favorite spot for a nap," says a man. A gentle breeze is blowing, and the park bench begins to feel drowsy, too.

A young man waits for his friend who is late.
"Let's meet in the park, at the white bench,"
they had agreed. "But now, where can she be?"

("Wait, who left a book on the bench?" the park worker wonders.)

「こうえんで　あおうね。
いつもの　しろい　ベンチでね。」って
やくそくしたのに，なかなか　こない　ともだち。
やくそく　わすれて　いないかなあ。

（おや，ベンチの　うえに　だれかの　わすれもの。）

Here comes a group of children running to the park.

This is the liveliest time of day.

"What are we going to play today?" asks one child.

"Let's talk it over."

こどもたちが　おおぜい　やって　きた。

こうえんが　いちばん　にぎやかに　なる　じかん。

「きょうは，なに　して　あそぶ？」

「そうだんしよう。しろい　ベンチに

みんな　あつまれー！」

しろい　ベンチは，おうちに　なる。おしろに　なる。　しまに　なる。ふねに　なる。
でんしゃに　なる。えきに　なる。　それから　ベンチにも　なる。

All of a sudden the white bench becomes a house.   Now it's a castle, then an island, now a boat.

Now a train. Then a station.   And then, it's even a park bench again!

23

Plip plop, plip plop . . .
"Uh-oh, here it comes," says the worker to himself.

Suddenly, it begins to rain.   Everyone runs for shelter.
Everyone except, of course, the white bench.

ぽつん，ぽつん，ぱららん……。
「おっ，ふって　きたかな。」

あめ，あめ，にわかあめ。
はしって，はしって，あまやどり。
きが　ぬれる。しばふが　ぬれる。
しろい　ベンチも　あめの　なか。

The rain has stopped.

Now the sky is bright.

The wet flowers and grass glisten.

"You're soaking wet," says the park worker

to the bench, as he gently wipes it dry.

"You're a fine bench in spite of your age," he says.

"I know you'll last for a long, long time."

あめが やんだ。 まぶしい そら。

はなにも, くさにも,

ひかる しずくが いっぱい。

「おやおや, びしょぬれだ。」

おじさんが ベンチを ふいて くれたよ。

「ずいぶん ふるく なったけど,

いい ベンチだからなあ。

まだまだ がんばって くれよ。」

こうえんの ゆうぐれ。 ちょっぴり かぜが つめたく なる。 「また あしたね。」って てを ふって,
こどもたちが かえって いく。 しろい ベンチも ゆうぐれの いろ。

Now the day is ending. The air becomes chilly.   Children wave to each other as they leave for home.
The white park bench is perfectly still in the twilight.

29

When the lights go on in the town, the worker's day is done.

"Good night, my dear white bench," he says.

"You must be very tired. I'll see you tomorrow."

He turns on the lights of his little motor cart and drives home.

まちに　あかりが　ともる　ころ,

おじさんの　しごとも　おしまいだ。

「さよなら,　しろい　ベンチ。

きょうも　いちにち　おつかれさま。

じゃ,　また　くるよ。」

ちいさな　くるまに　ライトを　つけて,

おじさんが　かえって　いく。

31

The park is covered with darkness.

Stars twinkle in the sky.

No one is here now, and the park is very still.

Under a tree sits a single white park bench.

Good night.

こうえんの　よる。

そらに　ほしが　きらり　きらり。

もう　だれも　いない　こうえんは，

とても　しずか。

きの　したに，しろい　ベンチが　ひとつ。

おやすみなさい。